VERY RUDE
LIMERICKS

By Stephen Cordwell

Limerick consultant: R. Pontin

See limerick on page 13

Grange BOOKS

See limerick on page 37

Grange
BOOKS

Very Rude
Limericks

By Stephen Cordwell

Limerick consultant: R. Pontin

Published by Grange Books
An imprint of Grange Books PLC
The Grange
Grange Yard
London
SEI 3AG

This edition published 1996

ISBN I 85627 504 3

Copyright © 1994. 1995, 1996 Regency House Publishing Limited

Printed in India.

Introduction

Limericks have a long and honourable history as a popular verse form. Their roots can be traced back to 14th century nursery rhymes and bawdy songs, and they gradually evolved to become an important aspect of traditional folk poetry.

By the 18th century, the limerick had become formalised as the verse structure we know today and had firmly established its position as the premier form of humorous, and usually rude, verse. Apart from brief periods when writers such as Edward Lear attempted to give the limerick form an acceptable literary face, it has steadfastly refused to behave politely.

It is almost impossible to establish the provenance of rude limericks. Their disreputable content discourages authors from appending their names, and the verses surface and circulate in uncensored anonymity. And therein lies much of their enduring appeal.

Anyone can employ this versatile literary form to launch their own rhymes without fear of reproof. Old favourites jostle with new inventions, often changing in the telling, as verses are paraded or traded in ribald recitations.

Perhaps your own secret offering might one day surface in a collection of this kind.

RUDE LIMERICKS

I wooed a stewed nude in Bermuda.
I was rude, but my God! she was ruder.
She said it was crude
To be wooed in the nude.
I pursued her, subdued her, and screwed her.

There was a young lady of Dover
Whose passion was such that it drove her
To cry when she came,
'Oh dear, what a shame!
Well now we just have to start over.'

There was a young fellow called Lancelot
Whose neighbours looked on him askance a lot.
Whenever he'd pass
A pretty young lass,
The front of his pants would advance a lot.

The spouse of a pretty young thing
Came home from the wars in the spring,
He was lame, but he came
With his dame like a flame -
A discharge is a wonderful thing.

There was an old man of Decatur
Who took out his trouser potater.
He tried at her dent
But when his thing bent,
He got down on his knees and he ate 'er.

There was a young girl called McBight
Who got drunk with her boyfriend one night.
She came to her bed
With a split maidenhead -
'Twas the last time she ever got tight.

Jill stitched up a thing of soft leather,
And topped off the end with a feather.
When she poked it inside her
She flew like a glider,
And gave up her lover forever.

A jaded young man from Darjeeling
Had a tool that reached up to the ceiling.
In the electric light socket
He'd stick it and rock it,
My word! What a wonderful feeling!

A young violinist from Rio
Was seducing a lady named Cleo.
As she slipped off her panties
She said, 'No andantes;
I want this *allegro con brio!'*

There was a young gigolo, Meek,
Who invented a lingual technique.
It drove women frantic,
Made them feel romantic,
And wore all the beard from his cheek.

An insatiable lady from Spain,
Had multiple sex on the brain.
She liked it again,
And again, and again,
And again, and again, and again.

There was a young maid named McDuff
With a lovely luxuriant muff.
In his haste to get in her
One eager beginner
Lost both of his balls in the rough.

There was a young man of Australia
Who painted his arse like a dahlia.
The drawing was fine,
The colour divine,
But the scent - alas - was a failure.

A vice both obscure and unsavoury
Kept the Bishop of Chester in slavery.
'Midst terrible howls
He deflowered young owls
In a crypt fitted out as an aviary.

A modern young lady named Hall
Went out to a birth control ball.
She was carrying pessaries
And other accessories,
But no one approached her at all.

A disgusting young man called McGill
Made his neighbours exceedingly ill
When they heard of his habits
Involving white rabbits
And a bird with a flexible bill.

There was a young fellow called Price
Who dabbled in all sorts of vice.
He loved virgins and boys
And mechanical toys,
And on Mondays he meddled with mice.

There was a young man from Racine
Who invented a knobbing machine.
Concave or convex,
It would suit either sex,
With attachments for those in between.

A lusty young ranger from Maine
With no woman for years had he lain.
He found sublimation
At a high elevation
In the crotch of a pine - God, the pain!

A young man with passions quite gingery
Tore a hole in his sister's best lingerie.
He spanked her behind
And made up his mind
To add incest to insult and injury.

There was a young woman called Gloria
Who was had by Sir Gerald Du Maurier,
By six other men,
Sir Gerald again,
And the band of the Waldorf-Astoria.

There was a young girl from Dundee
Who was raped by an ape in a tree.
The result was most horrid -
All arse and no forehead,
Three balls and an ill-groomed goatee.

A student of music from Sparta
Was a truly magnificent farter;
On the strength of one bean
He'd fart God Save the Queen,
And Beethoven's Moonlight Sonata.

There was a young girl called O'Clare
Whose body was covered in hair.
It was really quite fun
To probe with one's gun,
For the target might be anywhere.

A prudish young maiden from Florence
Wrote anti-sex pamphlets in torrents,
'Til a Spanish grandee
Got her hot with his knee,
And she burned all her works with abhorrence.

A lady by passion deluded
Found a hobo quite drunk and denuded,
And - fit as a fiddle,
And hot for a diddle -
She tied splints to his penis and screwed it.

To his girl said the lynx-eyed detective,
'Is my eyesight the least bit defective?
Has your east tit the least bit
The best of your west tit,
Or is it a trick of perspective?'

There was a young girl from Throgmorton
Who had one long tit and a short 'un.
To make up for that,
She'd a six foot wide twat,
And a fart like a 650 Norton.

Now Caroline, writer of verse,
Was laid low one day by the curse.
And her menstrual flow
Was a bit of a blow,
To the laundry, who'd seen nothing worse.

Jane met a young man for some action.
His foreplay gave her satisfaction.
They enjoined in coition
In the strangest position,
And his femur is now up in traction.

There was a young girl from Hoboken
Who claimed that her hymen was broken
From riding a bike
On a cobblestone spike,
But it really was broken from pokin'.

There was a young virgin from Bude
Whose proclivities were often viewed
With distrust by the males
For she'd fondle their rails,
But never would let them intrude.

There was a young lady from Dee
Who slept with each man she did see.
Should it come to a test
She wished to be best,
And practice makes perfect, you see.

There was a fair maid named Anheuser
Who said that no man could surprise her.
But Pabst took a chance,
Found Schlitz in her pants,
And now she is sadder Budweiser.

There was a young man from Rangoon
Who farted and filled a balloon.
The balloon went so high
That it stuck in the sky,
Which was tough for the Man in the Moon.

There was a young maid from Madrid
Who would open her legs for a quid.
But a handsome Italian
With balls like a stallion
Said he'd do it for nothing - and did.

There was an old king called Canute
Who was troubled by warts on his root.
He put acid on these,
And now when he pees,
He can finger his root like a flute.

There was a young maiden called Randall
Who caused quite a neighbourhood scandal
By walking out bare
To the main village square
And poking herself with a candle.

There was a young woman from Bicester
More willing by far than her sister.
The sister would giggle
And wriggle and jiggle,
But this one would come if you kissed her.

There was a young maiden called Flynn
Who thought fornication a sin,
But when she was tight
It seemed quite alright,
So everyone filled her with gin.

There was a young dentist called Stone
Who saw all his patients alone.
In a fit of depravity
He filled the wrong cavity,
Good Lord! How his practice has grown!

It is a delight here in Lancs.,
To walk up the green river banks.
One time, in the grass
I stepped on an arse,
And heard a young girl murmur, 'Thanks!'

An agreeable girl called Miss Doves
Likes to fondle the young men she loves.
She will use her bare fist
If the fellows insist
But she really prefers to wear gloves.

When a horny young curate in Leeds
Was discovered, one day in the weeds
Astride a young nun,
He cried, 'This is fun!
Far better than telling one's beads'.

There was a young woman called Hall
Wore a newspaper dress to a ball.
The dress caught on fire
And burned her entire,
Front page, sporting section,
and all.

Today's cinematic emporium
Is not just a visual sensorium,
But a highly effectual
Heterosexual
Mutual masturbatorium.

The limerick form is complex,
Its contents deal mainly with sex.
It burgeons with virgeons
And masculine urgeons,
And a wealth of erotic effex.

An astronomer slept in the sun,
Then woke with his fly quite undone.
He remarked, with a smile,
'Hoorah! A sundial!
And it's now a quarter past one.'

A girl of dubious nativity
Had an arse of extreme sensitivity.
When she sat on the lap
Of a German or Jap,
She could sense Fifth Column activity.

There once was a young man called Tensill
Whose organ was shaped like a pencil.
Anaemic, 'tis true,
But an excellent screw,
Inasmuch as the tip was prehensile.

There was an old man from Tagore
Whose tool was a yard long or more.
He supported the thing
In a surgical sling
To prevent it from scuffing the floor.

There was a young lady called Riddle
Who had an untouchable middle.
She acquired many friends
Because of her ends,
For it isn't the middle you diddle.

There was a young lady from Norway
Who hung by her heels from a doorway.
She said to her beau,
'Look at this, Joe,
I think I've discovered one more way!'

There once was a monk from Siberia
Whose morals were somewhat inferior.
He did to a nun
What he shouldn't have done,
And now she's a Mother Superior.

There once was a girl who begat
Three brats, by name Tat, Nat and Pat.
It was fun in the breeding
But hell in the feeding,
When she found there was no tit for Tat.

A zoologist's daughter from Ewing
Birthed a fine fritillary blue-wing.
Her father said, 'Flo,
What I want to know
Isn't whether, but what you've been screwing.'

There was a young maiden from Rheims
Who started to pee in four streams.
A friend poked around
And a fly-button found
Tightly wedged in her intimate seams.

A notorious hooker called Hearst
In the weakness of men is well versed.
Reads a sign by the head
Of her often used bed:
'The customer always comes first'.

There was an Oz tart from Naroo
Who filled her vagina with glue.
She said, with a grin,
'If they pay to get in,
They'll pay to get out of it too.'

A fellow from 'round Wookie Hole
Had a torrid affair with a mole.
Though surely a nancy,
He did rather fancy
Himself in the dominant role.

An attractive young girl from Des Moines
Had a very large sack full of coins.
The nickels and dimes
She had earned from the times
That she cradled young lads in her loins.

An unfortunate pirate called Bates
Liked to do the fandango on skates.
But he fell on his cutlass
Which rendered him nutless
And practically useless on dates.

A horny old miser called Fletcher
Grew tired of being known as a lecher.
In a spasm of meanness
He cut off his penis,
And now he regrets it, I bet'cha.

There was a young man of Hong Kong
Who sported a metre of prong.
It looked, when erect,
As one would expect,
When coiled, it did not seem so long.

The tool of a fellow called Randall
Shot sparks like a fine Roman candle.
His glorious stand
Produced colours quite grand,
But the girls found him too hot to handle.

An unfortunate chap from Port Said
Once fell down a toilet and died.
His unhappy mother
She fell down another;
And now they're interred side by side.

A preposterous King of Siam
Said, 'For women I don't give a damn.
But a fat-bottomed boy
Is my glee and my joy -
They call me a bugger - I am!'

There was a young man from Coblenz
Whose balls were quite simply immense:
It took forty draymen
A priest and three laymen
To transport them thither and hence.

When a woman in strapless attire
Found her breasts lifting higher and higher,
The guests formed a line
For the mantle was fine
And they all wished to stoke up the fire.

There once was an artist called Tensill
Whose tool was as sharp as a pencil.
He drove through an actress,
The sheet and the mattress,
And shattered the bedroom utensil.

A lascivious parson named Binns
Liked to talk of loose women and things.
But his secret desire
Was a boy in the choir
With a bottom like jelly on springs.

A lad of extremely high station
Was found by a prudish relation
Making love in a ditch
To - I won't say a bitch -
But a woman of no reputation.

There once was a gardener from Leeds
Who swallowed a packet of seeds.
Great tufts of grass
Sprouted out of his arse
And his balls were soon covered in weeds.

Said the Duchess of Chester at tea,
'Young man, do you fart when you pee?'
I replied with some wit,
'Do you belch when you shit?'
I think that was one up to me.

'I'll admit,' said a lady called Barr,
'That a penis is like a cigar;
But, in general, to people
A phallic church steeple
Is stretching the subject too far.'

A pooftah who lived in Khartoum
Took a lesbian up to his room,
And they argued all night
Over who had the right
To do what, and with what, and to whom.

An apprentice young stud from Purdue
Who was only just learning to screw,
Found he hadn't the knack,
He was much too far back -
In the right church, but in the wrong pew.

28

In spite of a fearsome disease
O'Reilly went down on his knees
Before altars of gods,
Whores, boys and large dogs -
And all this for very small fees.

A reckless young woman from France
Had no qualms about taking a chance,
But considered it crude
To get screwed in the nude,
So she always went home with damp pants.

A dancer who came from Darjeeling
Could perform with such sensuous feeling
There was never a sound
For miles around,
Save of fly buttons hitting the ceiling.

A rampant young knave from Ostend
Let a pretty girl play with his end.
She took hold of Rover,
And felt it all over,
And it did what she didn't intend.

I could hear the faint buzz of a bee
As it buried its sting deep in me.
Her arse it was fine
But you should have seen mine
In the shade of the old apple tree.

There was a Nabob of Madras
Whose balls were constructed of brass.
When jostled together
They played *Stormy Weather*,
And lightning shot out of his arse.

An astonishing tribe are the Sweenies,
Renowned for the length of their peenies.
The hair on their balls
Sweeps the floors of their halls,
But they don't care for women, the meanies.

A pretty young maid called Dalrymple
Whose sexual parts were so simple
That on peeking they found
Little more than a mound
In the centre of which was a dimple.

There was a young lady called Hilda
Who went for a walk with a builder.
He knew that he could,
And he should, and he would -
And he did - and it bloody near killed her!

A remarkable race are the Persians,
They do have so many diversions.
They screw the whole day
In the regular way,
And save up the night for perversions.

There was a young girl from Cornell
Whose nipples were shaped like a bell.
When you touched them they shrunk,
But when she got drunk,
They quickly got bigger than hell.

There was a fair maiden called Heather
Whose labia were fashioned in leather.
She made a strange noise,
Which attracted the boys,
By flapping the edges together.

'Last night,' said a lady called Ruth,
'In a long-distance telephone booth,
I enjoyed the perfection
Of an ideal connection -
I was screwed, if you must know the truth.'

A worried lad from Istanbul,
Discovered red marks on his tool.
Said the doctor, a cynic,
'Get out of my clinic,
And wipe off the lipstick, you fool!'

There was an old abbess quite shocked.
She found nuns where the candles were locked.
Said the abbess, 'You nuns
Should behave more like guns,
And never go off till you're cocked.'

There was a young lady called Astor
Who seldom let any get past her.
One night she got plenty
And finished at twenty.
One imagines that that ought to last 'er.

There was a young tyro called Fyffe
Who married the love of his life.
But imagine his pain
When he struggled in vain,
And just couldn't enter his wife.

There was a young man from Madras
Who was stuffing a maid in the grass.
But the tropical sun
Spoiled some of his fun
By singeing the hairs
on his arse.

There once was a maid from Sofia
Who succumbed to her lover's desire.
She said, 'It's a sin,
But now that it's in,
Could you push it a few inches higher?'

A forward young man with a fiddle
Asked a young fan, 'Do you diddle?'
She replied, 'Yes, I do,
But prefer it with two -
It's twice as much fun in the middle.'

There was a young woman called Dexter
Whose husband exceedingly vexed her,
For whenever they'd start
He'd let fly a great fart
With a blast that damn nearly unsexed her.

The priests of the temple of Isis
Used to offer up amber and spices,
Then nip round the shrine
And perform sixty-nine
And other unpardonable vices.

There was a young rent boy called Taylor
Who seduced a respectable sailor.
When they put him in jail
He settled the bail
By doing the same to the jailor.

An elderly bishop from Brest
Quite openly practised incest.
'My sisters and nieces
Are all dandy pieces,
And don't cost a *sou*,' he confessed.

A pathetic appellant in Reno
Was as chaste as the Holy Bambino,
For she'd married a slicker
Who much preferred liquor
And scorned her ripe maraschino.

An innocent maiden from Maine
Declared she'd a man on the brain.
But you knew from the view
Of the way her waist grew,
It was not on her brain he had lain.

A lady who hailed from Wadesmill
Sat down on a nearby mole's hill.
The resident mole
Stuck his head up her hole -
The lady's okay - but the mole's ill.

There was a young whore from Tashkent
Who commanded an immoral rent.
Day out and day in
She lay writhing in sin,
Giving thanks it was ten months to Lent.

I know of a story that's fraught
With disaster - of balls that got caught,
When a chap took a crap
In the woods, when a trap
Underneath ... Oh, I can't bear the thought.

An innocent maid from Penzance
Decided to take just one chance.
So she let herself go
In the lap of her beau,
And now all her sisters are aunts.

There once was a maiden from Thrace
Whose corsets grew too tight to lace.
Her mother said, 'Nelly,
There's things in your belly
That never got in through your face.'

A worn out young hooker from Rome
Was fatigued from her toes to her dome.
Eight soldiers came screwing,
But she said, 'Nothing doing;
One of you has to go home!'

There was a young girl from Eskdale
Who put up her sweet arse for sale.
For the sum of two bits
You could tickle her tits,
But a dollar would get you some tail.

A modest young maiden called Wilde
Sought to keep herself undefiled
By thinking of Jesus,
Contagious diseases,
And the bother of having a child.

The wife of a warrior Celt
Lost the key to her chastity belt.
She tried picking the lock
With an Ulsterman's cock,
And the next thing he knew, he was gelt.

There was a young lady called Ransom
Who was serviced three times in a hansom.
When she cried, 'Give me more!'
A voice from the floor
Said, 'My name is Simpson not Samson.'

There was an old maid from Bermuda
Who shot a marauding intruder.
It was not her ire
At his lack of attire,
But he reached for her jewels as he screwed her.

A girl called Alice from Dallas
Had yet to experience phallus.
She remained *virgo intacta,*
Because, *ipso facto,*
No phallus in Dallas fit Alice.

A loopy young fellow from Mecca,
Discovered a record from Decca,
Which he spun on his thumb
(These eccentrics are dumb)
While he needled the disc with his pecca.

Said a weary young fellow called Shea,
When his prick wouldn't stand for a lay,
'You must seize it and squeeze it,
And tease it and please it,
For Rome wasn't built in a day.'

When Angelico worked in cerise,
For an angel, he painted his niece.
In a heavenly trance
He whipped off her pants,
And erected a fine altar-piece.

The whang of a fellow called Grable
Was as pliant and long as a cable.
Each eve as he ate,
This suave reprobate
Would screw his wife under the table.

My grandfather adored his old tether
And loved tickling his balls with a feather.
But the thing he loved best
Out of all of the rest
Was jostling them gently together.

A eunuch who hailed from Port Said
Could enjoy a good romp in bed.
Nor could the Sultana
Detect from his manner
That he used a banana instead.

There was a young fellow called Dirk
Who dozed off one day after work.
He woke with a scream
When he had a wet dream,
And polished it off with a jerk.

There once was a Queen of Baroda
Who caused to be built a pagoda.
The walls of its halls
Were festooned with the balls
And the tools of the fools who bestrode her.

Anthropologists up with the Sioux
Cabled home for two punts, one canoe.
The answer next day,
Said, 'Girls on their way,
But what the hell's a "panoe"?'

There was a young stud from Missouri
Who fucked with astonishing fury,
'Til taken to court
For his vigorous sport,
And condemned by a poorly-hung jury.

A libidinous justice from Salem
Used to judge all the hookers and jail 'em.
But instead of a fine
He would stand them in line,
With his common-law tool to impale 'em.

There was a young couple called Kelly
Who had to live belly to belly,
For once, in their haste,
They used library paste
Instead of petroleum jelly.

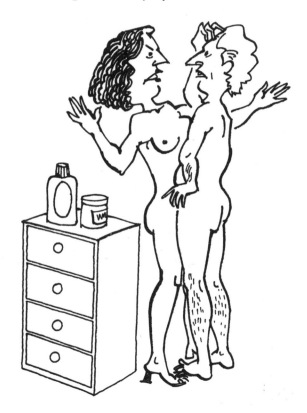

A randy young fellow called Reg
Was jerking off under a hedge.
The gardener drew near
With a large pruning shear,
And lopped off the edge of his wedge.

A prudish young woman from Ealing,
Professed to lack sexual feeling.
But a cynic called Boris
Just touched her clitoris,
And she had to be scraped off the ceiling.

The nipples of young Miss Hong Kong,
When excited are twelve inches long.
This embarrassed her lover
Who was pained to discover
She expected no less of his dong.

A considerate fellow named Tunney
Had a whizzer well worth any money.
When eased in half-way,
The girl's sigh made him say,
'Why the sigh?' 'For the rest of it, honey.'

There once was a fellow named Brink
Who possessed an extremely tart dink.
To sweeten it some,
He soaked it in rum,
Now he's driven his girlfriend to drink.

An adventurous lady from Troy
Invented a new kind of joy:
She sugared her quim,
And frosted the rim,
And then had it sucked by a boy.

There was a man from Bhoghat,
Whose arse cheeks were terribly fat.
They had to be parted
Whenever he farted,
And propped wide apart when he shat.

A handsome young laundress called Spangle
Had tits tilting up at an angle.
'They may tickle my chin,'
She said, with a grin,
'But at least they stay clear of the mangle.'

A singular lady called Grace
Had eyes in a very strange place.
She could sit on the hole
Of a mouse or a mole
And stare the beast straight in the face.

The Grenadiers are very strange bods.
While marching the park, formed in squads,
They saw two nude statues
From three-quarter prat views,
Which noticeably stiffened their rods.

A copper from Old Clapham Junction,
Whose organ had long ceased to function,
Deceived his dear wife
For the rest of her life
With the aid of his constable's truncheon.

A languid young man from Racine
Wasn't weaned until nearly sixteen.
He said, 'I'll admit
There's no milk in the tit,
But think of the fun it has been.'

There was a young Scot from Dumfries
Who said to his girl, 'If you please,
It would give me great joy
If with this you could toy,
Then pay some attention to these.'

My wife is an amorous soul,
On fire for a young athlete's pole.
She called her new chauffeur
Her sexual gopher,
And, boy, did he go for her hole!

There once was a fellow, McNamiter
With a prick of prodigious diameter.
But it wasn't the size
Gave girls a surprise,
But his rhythm - iambic pentameter.

An elegant fellow, young Saul;
He was able to bounce either ball.
He could stretch 'em and snap 'em,
And juggle and clap 'em,
Which earned him the plaudits of all.

RUDER LIMERICKS

A lonely old lady called May
Used to stroll in the park 'cross the way.
There she met a young man
Who fucked her and ran -
Now she goes to the park every day.

'At a séance,' said a fellow called Post,
'I was being sucked off by a ghost;
Someone switched on the lights
And there, in silk tights,
On his knees, was old Basil mine host.'

An ancient but jolly old bloke
Once picked up a lass for a poke;
He wore her plum out
With his fucking about,
Then he shit in her shoe for a joke.

A student who hailed from St John's
Badly wanted to bugger the swans.
'Oh no,' said the porter,
'Please bugger my daughter,
Them swans is reserved for the Dons.'

A lecher who lived in Bombay
Had fashioned a cunt out of clay.
The heat from his prick
Fired the damn thing to brick,
And abraded his foreskin away.

An ancient old whore named McGee
Was just the right sort for a spree.
Said she, 'For a fuck
I charge half a buck,
And throw in the arsehole for free.'

A well-endowed fellow called Danny
The size of whose prick was uncanny,
Made his wife, the poor dear,
Take it into her ear,
And it came out the hole in her fanny.

An elderly chap from Tagore
Wished to try out his cook as a whore.
He used Bridget's twidget
To fidget his digit,
And now she won't cook any more.

There was a young squaw of Chokdunt
Who had a collapsible cunt.
Though it had many uses,
It made no papooses,
But fitted both giant and runt.

A pretty wife dwelling in Tours
Asked much of her faithful amour.
But her husband said, 'No!
On I just cannot go!
My bollocks are dragging the floor.'

A young matelot new to Brighton
Remarked to his girl, 'You've a tight one.'
She replied, ''Pon my soul,
You're in the wrong hole -
There's plenty of room in the right one.'

There was an old roué named Tucker
Who, instructing a novice cock-sucker,
Said, 'Don't stretch out your lips
Like an elephant's hips,
Us chaps like it best if you pucker.'

An Arab called Abou ben Adhem
Thus cautioned a travelling madam,
'I suffer from crabs
As do most us A-rabs.'
'It's alright,' said madam, 'I've had 'em.'

There was a sweet maiden called Dowd
Whom a young lecher groped in a crowd.
But the thing that most vexed her
Was when he stood next her
He said, 'How's your cunt?' right out loud.

There was a lascivious wench
Whom nothing could ever make blench.
She'd insert a man's pole
In just any old hole,
And she'd bugger, fuck, jerk-off and French.

There was a young girl from Detroit
Who at screwing was very adroit.
She could squeeze her vagina
To a pin-point, or finer,
Or open it out like a quoit.

The appeal of a whore in Bengot
Was the absence of hair on her twat.
It was smooth as a dream,
Not through shaving or cream,
But through all the fucking she got.

An eager young fellow from Norway,
Tried to jerk himself off in a sleigh.
But the air was so frigid
It froze his balls rigid
And all he produced was frappé.

There was a sweet lady who said,
As her new beau climbed into her bed,
'I'm tired of this stunt
That they do with one's cunt,
You can slip up my bottom instead.'

There was a señora from Spain
Whose appearance was mightily plain,
But her quim had a pucker
That made the men fuck her,
Again and again and again.

Alas, the poor Duchess of Kent!
Her cunt is amazingly bent.
The poor thing doth stammer,
'I need a sledgehammer
To pound a man into my vent!'

A worn-out old hooker called Tupps
Was heard to confess in her cups;
'The height of my folly
Was fucking a collie,
But I got a fine price for the pups.'

A hooker of note called Miss Flux
Could command at least two hundred bucks.
But for that she would suck you,
And jerk-off, and fuck you;
The whole thing was simply de luxe.

A frustrated young laundress of Lamas
Would imagine great amorous dramas
For the spots she espied
Dried and hardened inside
The pants of the vicar's pyjamas.

An incorrigible clown from St James
Indulged in the jolliest games;
He lighted the rim
Of his grandmother's quim,
And guffawed as she pissed through the flames.

There was a notorious seaman
Who with ladies was quite a young demon.
In peace or in war,
At sea or on shore,
He was liberal and free with his semen.

There was a fair lady at sea
Who said, 'How it hurts me to pee.'
'I see,' said the mate,
'That accounts for the state
Of the captain, the purser, and me.'

There was a young stud from Glenchasm
Who had a stupendous orgasm.
In the midst of his thrall
He burst both his balls,
And covered an acre with plasm.

A very young maid from Peru
Had nothing whatever to do,
So she sat on the stairs
And counted cunt hairs -
Five thousand, six hundred and two.

There was a fair maiden whose joys
Were achieved with remarkable poise.
She would reach her orgasm
With scarcely a spasm,
And could fart without making a noise.

Two innocent ladies from Grimsby
Inquired, 'Of what use can our quims be?
The hole in the middle
Is so we can piddle,
But for what can the hole near the rims be?'

There was a most versatile whore,
As expert behind as before.
For five quid you could view her,
And bugger and screw her,
As she stood on her head on the floor.

Said an urgent young sailor called Micky,
As his girl eyes his stiff, throbbing dicky,
'Pet, my leave's almost up,
And I need a good tup -
Bend over, I'll slip you a quickie.'

A miserly man named McEwan
Inquired, 'Why bother with screwing?
It's safer and cleaner
To polish your *wiener*,
And besides, you can see what you're doing.'

There was a young fellow from Datchet
Who lopped off his prick with a hatchet.
He sent it to Whitely,
With a note wrote politely,
And ordered a cunt that would match it.

A lesbian lady named Annie
Wished to be less girly, more manny,
So she whittled a pud
Of gnarly old wood,
And let it protrude from her cranny.

There was an experienced whore
Who knew all the coital lore.
She said, 'Though it pain us,
Men opt for my anus,
So now I don't fuck any more.'

A certain young fellow from Buckingham
Stood on the old bridge at Ruckingham
Watching the stunts
Of the cunts in the punts
And the tricks of the pricks that were
fucking 'em.

A well-endowed man from Toledo
Was cursed with excessive libido.
To bugger and screw,
Take fellatio too,
Were the three major points of his credo.

There was a young lady called Moore
Who, while not quite precisely a whore,
Could not miss the chance
To whip off her pants
To compare a man's stroke with her bore.

Old nymphomaniacal Alice
Used a dynamite stick for a phallus.
They found her vagina
In downtown Regina,
And her arsehole in Buckingham Palace.

An indelicate lady called Bruce,
She captured her man with a ruse:
She packed up her fuselage
With a good, viscous mucilage,
And he never could prise himself loose.

There was a young stud in Madrid
Who got fifty good fucks for a quid.
When they said, 'Aren't you faint?'
He replied, 'No, I ain't,
But I don't feel as well as I did.'

There was a young monk from Tibet,
And this is the strangest one yet -
His prick was so long,
So pointed and strong,
He could bugger six Greeks *en brochette*.

The wife of a sportsman called Chuck
Found her married life clean out of luck.
Her husband played hockey
Without wearing a jockey,
Now he ain't what it takes for a fuck.

A harlot from Epping-on-Tyne
Used to peddle her arse down the line.
She first got a crown,
But her value went down -
Now she'll fuck you for ten pence or nine.

An elegant roué called Scott
Took a horny young maid to his yacht.
But too lazy to rape her,
He made darts of brown paper,
Which he languidly flew at her twat.

'It's dull in Duluth, Minnesota,
Of spunk there is not an iota,'
Complained Alice to Joe,
Who tried not to show
That he yawned as he poked with his bloater.

There was a young pervert from Mayence
Who fucked his own arse in defiance
Not only of habit
And morals but - dammit -
Most of the known laws of science.

A phobic young virgin called Flynn
Shouted before she gave in:
'It isn't the deed,
Or the fear of the seed,
But the big worm that's shedding it's skin!'

When Theocritus guarded his flock
He piped in the shade of a rock.
It is said that his Muse
Was one of the ewes
With a twat like a pink hollyhock.

It's recorded that Emperor Titius
Had a preference for pleasures most vicious.
He took two of his nieces
And fucked them to pieces,
And thought it completely delicious.

'It's been a very fine day,'
Yawned Lady McDougal McKay.
'Three cherry tarts,
At least twenty farts,
Two shits and a bloody good lay.'

'Doc, I took your advice,' said McKnop,
'And made the wife get up on top.
Got her bouncing about,
But it kept falling out,
And the kids, much amused, made us stop.'

The Coroner reported, in Preston,
'The verdict is anal congestion.
I found an eight-ball
On a sailmaker's awl
Halfway up the Commander's intestine.'

A cricketing fan called Miss Glend
Was the home-team's supporter and friend.
But for her a big match
Never fired up her snatch
Like a bat with two balls up her end.

A newly-wed couple called Goshen
Spent their honeymoon sailing the ocean,
Through eighty positions,
Their complex coitions
Demonstrated their fucking devotion.

Fuck me quick, fuck me deep, fuck me oft,
In the bog, in the bath, in the loft,
Up my arse, up my cunt,
From behind, from in front,
With your best, stiffest stand, nothing soft.

A woman who lived in a spinney
Had a cunt that could bark, neigh or whinny.
The hunting set hopped her,
Fucked, buggered, then dropped her
When the pitch of her organ went tinny.

The Vicar of Dunstan St Just
Consumed with irregular lust,
Raped the Bishop's prize fowls,
Buggered four startled owls
And a little green lizard, that bust.

There was a young girl named Priscilla,
Who flavoured her cunt with vanilla.
The taste was so fine,
Men and beasts stood in line,
But she called it a day with Godzilla.

There was a young lady from Cheam
Crept into the vestry unseen.
She ripped off her knickers,
Likewise the vicar's,
And rammed in the episcopal bean.

There was a young maid from Cape Cod
Who dreamed she was sleeping with God.
'Twas not the Almighty
Who pulled up her nightie,
'Twas Roger the lodger, the sod!

A Sunday school student in Mass
Soon rose to the top of the class,
By getting things right,
And sleeping the night
With his tongue up the clergyman's ass.

There was a young lady called Blunt
Who possessed a rectangular cunt.
She learned, for diversion,
Posterior perversion,
As no one could fit her in front.

An innovative fellow called Hunt
Trained his prick to perform a neat stunt:
This versatile spout
Could be turned inside out
Like a glove, and be used as a cunt.

There was a young widow from Kent
With a cunt of enormous extent,
And so deep and so wide,
The acoustics inside
Formed an echo whenever you spent.

A grubby young harlot called Schwartz
Had a cunt that was covered in warts.
They tickled so nice
She'd command a high price
From the blokes in the summer resorts.

A young lass from North Carolina,
Had a most capricious vagina:
To startle the fucker
'Twould suddenly pucker,
And whistle the chorus of *Dinah*.

A maiden who dwelled in Palm Springs
Had her maidenhead torn into strings
By a hideous Kurd,
And although it's absurd,
When the wind blows through it, it sings.

A Paris-based artist named Sayer
As a cubist was really quite fair.
He searched all his life
To find him a wife
Possessed of a cunt that was square.

An indolent fellow called Blood
Made his fortune by being a stud,
With a fifteen inch whang
And bollocks that clang
And a load like the Biblical flood.

There once was a well-blessed young Hindu
Much admired in the towns that he'd been to
By the women he knows,
Who wriggle their toes
At the tricks he can make his foreskin do.

There was a young lady from Natchez
Who was fully equipped with two snatches.
She often cried, 'Shit!
I'd give either tit
For a man with equipment that matches.'

An unusual woman called Creek
Had taught her vagina to speak.
It was frequently liable
To quote from the Bible,
But when fucking - not even a squeak!

A tip for you jaded old souls:
Try changing the usual roles.
The backwards position
Is nice for coition
And offers the choice of two holes.

Old Louis Quatorze was 'ot sterf.
'E tired of zat game, blindman's berf,
Upended his mistress,
Kissed 'ers as she kissed 'is,
And zo taught ze world *soixante-neuf.*

There once was a lass from Samoa
Who plugged up her cunt with a boa.
This weird contraceptive
Was very effective
To all but the spermatazoa.

Another young maid from New York
Chose to plug up her cunt with a cork.
A woodpecker or two
Made the grade, it is true,
But it utterly baffled the stork.

A pox-ridden lady called Rix
Was enamoured of sucking large pricks.
One fellow she took
Was a doctor called Crook
Now he's in one hell of a fix.

There was a young fellow from Kent
Whose tool was amazingly bent.
To save himself trouble
He put it in double,
And instead of coming, he went.

A young man who once lived in Briggen
Went to sea to recover from frigging.
But after a week
As they climbed the forepeak
He buggered the mate in the rigging.

An unusual chap, I should mention,
Has a hair-lined lower intestine.
Though exceedingly fine
In the buggery line,
It's notoriously poor for digestin'.

A cruel old whore from Albania
Hated men with a terrible mania.
With a clench and a squirm
She would pinch back the sperm,
Then roll on her front and distain ya.

An adventurous lad from Kildare
Was fucking a girl on the stair.
The bannister broke,
But he doubled his stroke
And finished her off in mid-air.

A timid young maiden from Thrace
Said, 'Darling! That's not the right place!'
So he gave her a smack,
And did on her back
What he couldn't have done face to face.

There once was a fellow called Ziegal
Who decided to bugger a beagle,
But just as he came,
A voice called his name,
Saying, 'Now me, but you know it's illegal.'

The desperate Vicar of Goring
Drilled a suitable hole in the flooring.
He lined it all round,
Then gently he ground.
It's neater and cheaper than whoring.

An intrepid young Frenchman called Rhemmes
Was attempting to fuck on a tandem.
At the peak of the make
She slammed on the brake,
And scattered his semen at random.

A bestial girl from Decatur
Was fucked by an old alligator.
No one ever knew
How she relished that screw,
For after he fucked her, he ate her.

There once was a big boy called Bowen
Whose penis kept growin' and growin'.
It grew so tremendous,
So heavy and pendulous,
'Twas no good for fuckin' - just showin'.

That wicked old Sappho from Greece
Said, 'What makes me feel really at peace
Is to have my pudenda
Rubbed hard by the enda
The snub little nose of my niece.'

An ambitious young woman in Reno,
Lost most of her money on keeno.
But she lay on her back
And opened her crack,
And now she owns all the casino.

A sensible bounder called Frisk
Had a method of screwing that's brisk.
The idea was: 'If
The bitch has the syph,
This way I'm reducing the risk.'

An impoverished fellow from Yale
Had a face that was notably pale.
He spent his vacation
In self-masturbation
Because of the high cost of tail.

An inquisitive chap from Lapland
Was informed that fucking was grand.
But at his first trial
He said with a smile,
'I've had the same feeling by hand.'

An unusual nurse from Japan
Lifted men by their pricks to the pan.
A trick of jujitsu,
And either it shits you,
Or makes you feel more of a man.

A grumpy and gloomy old Druid,
A pessimist, if he but knew it,
Said, 'The world's on the skids
And I think having kids
Is a waste of good seminal fluid.'

A prudish young maiden called Rose
Is particular how men propose.
When they say, 'Intercourse?'
She answers. 'Of course,'
But to 'Fuck?' she just turns up her nose.

A versatile athlete called Grimmon
Developed a new way of swimmin':
'Twas a marvellous trick,
He would row with his prick,
And attracted loud cheers from the women.

There was a hill farmer from Nant
Whose behaviour was barely gallant,
For he fucked all his dozens
Of nieces and cousins,
In addition, of course, to his aunt.

An elderly lecher from York
Had a prick that was dry as a cork.
While attempting to screw
He split it in two,
And now his poor tool is a fork.

Said an awfully innocent siren,
'Young sailors are cute - I must try one!'
She came home in the nude,
Stewed, screwed, and tattooed
With lewd pictures and verses from Byron.

The well-known orthographer, Chisholm,
Caused a lexicographical schism
When he asked to know whether
'Twere known which was better
To use - G or J - to spell jism.

All the she-apes avoided King Kong
For his prick was horrendously long.
But a carefree giraffe
Quaffed his yard and a half,
With a gargling outbreak of song.

The king gave a lesson in class,
When he was once fondling a lass.
When she used the word 'damn',
He chided, 'Please ma'am,
Keep a more civil tongue in my arse.'

There was a young man from Arras
Lying quiet and still on the grass.
With a sudden, huge lunge
He bent like a sponge,
And stuck his prick up his own arse.

'There surely must be a trick to it,'
Said a Peeping Tom watching all through it.
'While he's locked in that ring,
I will whip out my thing,
And polish it while I review it.'

On the tits of a barmaid from Sale
Were tattooed all the prices of ale.
And on her behind
For the sake of the blind,
Was the same list of prices in Braille.

There was a young man from Devizes
Whose balls were of different sizes.
The left one was small,
Almost no ball at all,
And the right one was large and won prizes.

There was a young girl from Dundee
Who went down to the river to swim.
And a man in a punt,
Stuck an oar in her eye,
And now she wears glasses, you see.

There once was a dancer from Exeter
So pretty that men craned their necks at her.
But some, more depraved,
Unzipped them and waved
The distinguishing marks of their sex at 'er.

Midsummer-Night's Dream's like a fever
When good old Bottom the Weaver,
Slipped his huge member out,
And up the Queen's spout
Without her knowing.
Now who would believe her?

An old couple at Eastertide
Were having a bit when he died.
The wife for a week
Sat tight on his peak,
And bounced up and down as she cried.

A geologist called Doctor Robb
Was perturbed by the urge in his knob,
So he put down his pick
And jerked off his wick,
Then calmly went on with his job.

Growing tired of her husband's great mass,
A young bride inserted some glass.
The cock of her hubby
Is now short and stubby,
And the wife can piss out of her arse.

There was an old leper from Bosham
Who took out his bollocks to wash 'em.
His wife said, 'Jack,
If you don't put 'em back,
I'll jump on your scrotum and squash 'em.'

There were two rampant men of Jahore
Who buggered and fucked the same whore.
But the partition split
And both jism and shit
Leaked out in a gush on the floor.

A young lady got married in Chester,
Her mother she kissed and she blessed her.
Says she, 'You're in luck,
He's a bloody good fuck,
For I had him myself down in Leicester.'

I love her in her evening gown,
I love her in her nightie,
When moonlight flits
Across her tits -
Jesus Christ Almighty!

There was a young fellow called Runyon,
Whose penis developed a bunion.
With every erection,
This painful infection,
Gave off a strong odour of onion.

An enormously fat girl, Regina,
Employed a young water diviner,
To play a slick trick
With his prick as a stick,
To help her locate her vagina.

There was a young man, Mr Rub-a-dub,
Who belonged to the Suck, Fuck and Bugger
Club,
But the joy of his life
Were the tits of his wife -
One real, and one India-rubber bub.

A lesbian lady called Maud
Did well in the WACS by a fraud.
Her tongue, quite infernal,
Slipped into the colonel,
And now she's a major, By Gawd!

A caddy called Tommy the Tough
Had an heiress way out in the rough.
He said, 'Let's not fuck,
Let's you and me suck.'
And he buried his head in her muff.

There was a young fellow called Howell
Who buggered himself with a trowel.
The triangular shape
Was conducive to rape,
And easily cleaned with a towel.

There once was a Cambridge B.A.
Who pondered the problem all day
Of what there would be.
If c-u-n-t
Were divided by c-o-c-k.

DISGUSTING LIMERICKS

A libidinous fellow - a banker,
Had bubo, itch, pox, and a chancre.
He got all the four
From a dirty old whore.
He's reduced to just being a wanker.

A ne'er-do-well fellow from Kent
Had his wife fuck the landlord for rent.
But as her cunt dried,
The landlord's lust died,
And now they camp out in a tent.

There was a young man from Peru
Whose lineage was noble all through.
It's surely not crud,
For not only his blood
But even his semen was blue.

A lascivious lady from Sidney
Could take fucking right up to her kidney.
But a chap from Quebec
Shoved it up to her neck.
He had a real beauty, now didn't he?

A torrid young man from Stamboul
Had so hot and tumescent a tool
That each female crater
Explored by this satyr
Seemed almost unpleasantly cool.

There once was a miserly knave
Who kept a dead whore in a cave.
'It takes lots of pluck
To have a cold fuck,
But think of the money I save!'

I recall an old man from Duluth
Whose cock was shot off in his youth.
He fucked with his nose
And his fingers and toes,
And he came through a hole in his tooth.

We knows three young ladies from Cuxham,
And whenever we meets 'em, we fucks 'em.
When that game grows stale
We sits on a rail,
We pulls out our pricks, and they sucks 'em.

A lady who thought sex a treat
Thought a gang-bang would make life complete.
Fifteen men and a dog
All went the whole hog,
And she left a snail trail down the street.

A pervert who lived in Khartoum
Was exceedingly fond of the womb.
He thought nothing finer
Than a woman's vagina,
And kept three or four in his room.

The very same man from Khartoum,
Lured an innocent girl to her doom.
He not only fucked her,
He buggered and sucked her
And left her to pay for the room.

A squeamish young student named Brand
Adored caressing his gland.
But he viewed with distaste
The gelatinous paste
That it left in the palm of his hand.

Thus spake the old Bey from Algiers,
'I've been whoring around for long years,
And my language is blunt:
A cunt is a cunt
And fucking is fucking.'(Loud cheers).

A lascivious fellow called Lees
Loved to give his poor cock a long squeeze.
This continual friction
Made real sex a mere fiction,
But the callous hung down to his knees.

Have you heard the sad tale of young Lockett?
He was blown off his feet by a rocket.
The force of the blast
Blew his balls up his arse,
And his penis was found in his pocket.

There was a young writer called Twain
Whose cock had a sinister stain.
And when he bent down,
You could see it was brown,
And was said to wash off in the rain.

An experienced hooker, Arlene,
Said, 'Give me a lad of eighteen.
His pecker gets harder,
There's more cream in his larder,
And he fucks with a vigour obscene.'

'My back aches, my penis is sore.
I simply can't fuck any more.
I'm dripping with sweat,
And you haven't come yet,
And, my God! it's quarter past four!'

There was an old lecher from Critch,
Had the syph and the clap and the itch.
His name was McNabs
And he also had crabs,
That dirty old son-of-a-bitch.

An ancient old tart from Silesia,
Said she, 'As my cunt doesn't please ya,
You might as well come
Up my slimy old bum,
But beware that my tapeworm don't seize ya.'

A similar tart from Marseilles,
Douched with the new rotary spray.
Said she, 'Ah, that's better
I've found that French letter
That's been missing since Armistice Day.'

An indelicate fellow from Ealing,
Was devoid of all sociable feeling.
When a sign on the door
Read, 'Don't shit on the floor',
He jumped up and shat on the ceiling.

An unwashed young girl from the Klondike
Had a body that was worth quite a long hike.
And her face isn't bad,
Yet she's never been had,
'Cos her cunt has a smell very cod-like.

A horrid small girl in Madrid,
A most insensitive kid,
Told her Auntie Louise
That her cunt smelled of cheese,
And the worst of it was that it did!

There once was a maiden from Arden
Who sucked off her man in the garden.
He said, 'Darling Flo,
Where does my sperm go?'
She replied, (swallow hard) -
'Beg your pardon?'

There was a young novice called Bell
Who didn't like cunt all that well.
He would finger and fuck one,
But never could suck one,
He just couldn't get used to the smell.

A scrofulous woman from Chester,
Said to the man who undressed her,
'I think you will find
That it's better behind,
The front is beginning to fester.'

A detective called Ellery Queen
Had olfactory powers so keen,
He can tell at a flash
By sniffing a gash
Who the previous tenant has been.

A willing Scots lass called McFargle,
Without coaxing and such ary-bargle,
Would suck a man's pud
Just as hard as she could,
And save up the sperm for a gargle.

A considerate stripper called Jane
Donned a pelmet of thin cellophane.
When asked why she wore it
She said, 'I abhor it,
But my cunt juice would spatter like rain.'

There once was a miserly knave
Who kept a dead whore in a cave.
He said, 'I'll admit
I'm a bit of a shit,
But think of the money I save!'

A scandal involving an oyster
Sent the Countess of Clewes to a cloister,
She preferred it, in play,
To the Count, they all say,
Being longer, and stronger, and moister.

There once was a miserly knave
Who kept a dead whore in a cave.
He said, 'It's disgusting,
But only needs dusting,
And think of the money I save!'

Another fellow - called Dave -
When he found that dead whore in the cave,
Said, 'I'll go first,
And if she doesn't burst,
I'll come to the entrance and wave.'

When his friend's turn came to pass,
He took in a bundle of grass
To make a soft buffer
To protect, when he stuffed her,
His prick if it poked through her arse.

Yet one more, whose excitable gland
Made him think this adventure was grand,
Thought fucking cold meat
An unusual treat,
'Til a tit came adrift in his hand.

There was a young man from Nantucket
Whose cock was so long he could suck it.
He said with a grin,
As he wiped off his chin,
'If my ear was a cunt I would fuck it.'

There was a young vicar of Eltham
Who wouldn't fuck girls, but he felt 'em.
In lanes he would linger
And play stinky finger,
And moan with delight when he smelt 'em.

There was a fair maiden called Grace
Who took all she could in her face,
But a well-endowed lad
Gave her all that he had,
And blew tonsils all over the place.

A liberal lass from Blackheath
Chose to fuck an old man with her teeth.
She complained that he stunk,
Not so much from the spunk,
But his arsehole was just underneath.

A weakling who lacked protoplasm
Sought to give his young wife an orgasm,
But his tongue jumped the gap
'Twixt the front and the back,
And got pinched in a bad anal spasm.

An Admiral of old called Horatio
Was inordinately fond of fellatio.
He kept accurate track
Of the boys he'd attack,
And called it his cock-sucking ratio.

If you're speaking of actions immoral,
Then how about giving the laurel
To doughty Queen Esther,
No three men could best her -
One fore, one aft, and one oral.

A price-conscious hooker called Annie
Whose tariff was fair, but quite canny:
A pound for a fuck,
Fifty pence for a suck,
And two bob for a feel of her fanny.

A vicar advised Barbara Lennin,
'A kiss of your cunt isn't sinnin'.'
And he stuck to his story
'Til he tasted the gory
And menstruous state that she was in.

An unusual man from Kutki
Could wank himself off with one eye.
For a while, though, he pined
When his eyeball declined
To function because of a stye.

A horny young fellow called Rick
Liked to feel a girl's hand on his prick.
He taught them to fool
With his tumescent tool,
'Til his well-polished member was sick.

A tidy young girl from Berlin
Chose to eke out a living through sin.
Although she loved fucking,
She much preferred sucking,
And wiped off the pricks with her chin.

There was a young girl called Dolores,
Whose cunt was all covered in sores.
The dogs in the street
Used to snap at the meat,
That hung in green gobs from her drawers.

There was a young fellow from Perth -
The dirtiest bugger on earth.
When his wife was confined
He crept up behind,
And swallowed the whole afterbirth.

There was an old Bey from Calcutta
Who greased up his arsehole with butter.
Instead of the roar
Which emitted before,
Came a soft, oleaginous flutter.

There was a young gaucho called Bruno
Who said, 'There's one thing that I do know.
A woman is fine,
A boy is divine,
But a llama is *numero uno*.

There was a young man from Nantucket
Took a pig to a thicket to fuck it.
Said the pig, 'No, I'm queer,
Get away from my rear,
Just come to the front and I'll suck it.'

There was an old man from Corfu
Who fed upon cunt-juice and spew.
When he couldn't get that
He ate what he shat,
And bloody good shit he shat too.

Said an overworked hooker called Randells,
Of the dozens of men that she handles,
'When I get this busy
My cunt gets so jizzy,
That it runs down my legs like wax candles.'

A vigorous whore from Warsaw,
Fucked all of her customers raw.
She would thump with her rump,
And punt with her cunt,
And suck every prick that she saw.

There was an old hooker from Grotten
Who plugged her diseased cunt with cotton.
For it was no myth
That she had the syph -
She stunk, and her arsehole was rotten.

There was a young lady from Readin'
Who got pox'd and the virus was spreadin'.
Her cunt layers each day
Kept sloughing away,
Until you could shove your whole head in.

A cardinal living in Rome
Had a Renaissance bath in his home.
He would savour the nudes
As he worked up his moods,
In emulsions of semen and foam.

A lewd Northumbrian Druid
Had a mind so filthy and lewd,
He woke from a trance
With his hand in his pants
On a lump of cold seminal fluid.